NORTHERN IRELAND

NORTHERN IRELAND

Peace in Our Time?

Ted Gottfried

The Millbrook Press
Brookfield, Connecticut

Published by The Millbrook Press, Inc.
2 Old New Milford Road
Brookfield, Connecticut 06804
www.millbrookpress.com

Library of Congress Cataloging-in-Publication Data
Gottfried, Ted.
Northern Ireland : peace in our time? / Ted Gottfried.
p. cm. — (Headliners)
Includes bibliographical references (p.) and index.
Summary: Presents the political history of Ireland, including the effects of
British rule, and the struggle to reconcile differing visions of the future of
the six counties of Northern Ireland.
ISBN 0-7613-2252-3 (lib. bdg.)
1. Northern Ireland—History—Juvenile literature. 2. Political violence—
Northern Ireland—Juvenile literature. 3. Social conflict—Northern Ireland—
Juvenile literature. 4. Peace movements—Northern Ireland—Juvenile
literature. [1. Northern Ireland—History. 2. Ethnic relations—Northern
Ireland. 3. Political violence. 4. Peace movements—Northern Ireland.]
I. Title. II. Series.
DA990.U46 G65 2002 941.6—dc21 2001042557

Contents

Chapter 1

Seeds of Turmoil

They call it Bloody Sunday. It was the defining moment in what the people of Northern Ireland refer to as "The Troubles." On January 30, 1972, the Northern Ireland Civil Rights Association organized a march of some 30,000 people in Derry to protest Catholics being held in jail without trial. When the march was blocked by the British army, the people regrouped in the Bogside neighborhood. Suddenly armored cars appeared. British paratroopers armed with combat rifles moved in. They began clubbing the demonstrators.

Shots rang out. People began to fall. There were screams. Rapid gunfire poured into the unarmed crowd. It went on for fifteen minutes. When it was over, thirteen people were dead. Seventeen were wounded, and one of them died later. A man photographed as he was taken into custody by the British was later found shot dead.

Opposite:
Demonstrators in Derry, Ireland, on January 30, 1972, faced British soldiers armed with guns, water cannons, and tear gas.

Early History of Ireland

Long a land of conflict between Irish and English, Catholics and Protestants, Northern Ireland is a saucer-shaped British-ruled territory consisting of six counties covering 5,452 square miles (14,298 square kilometers) in the northeast corner of the island of Ireland. Of the roughly 1.7 million inhabitants, about 58 percent are Protestant and 42 percent Roman Catholic. Once, Northern Ireland was part of the Catholic nation of Ireland, but the country was divided in 1920. Before then the history of Northern Ireland was part of the history of the entire island, a land so lush and green that it was known as the Emerald Isle, a small island lying off the coast of the larger island of England, which itself lay off the coast of the continent of Europe.

Evidence of human beings on the island goes back to 6000 B.C. These people were hunters and gatherers who over the centuries developed into farmers and set up villages. Between 600 and 150 B.C., they were conquered by Gaelic invaders from Western Europe. The Gaels, also known as Celts, turned Ireland into a loosely knit nation.

In the fifth century A.D., Saint Patrick introduced Christianity into Ireland. During the sixth and seventh centuries, Irish monasteries were notable centers of learning. While most of Europe struggled through the Dark Ages, religious art and illustrated manuscripts like the renowned Book of Kells established Irish culture.

The Conquest of Ireland

In the twelfth century Anglo-Norman barons from England began to raid Ireland. They seized Irish lands, and their ownership was later backed up by an army led by King Henry II of England. In this way Ireland became a colony of England with a government that was Irish but subject to British rule.

Up to the mid-sixteenth century, both the Irish and the English were Catholics. However, when Pope Clement VII refused to grant King Henry VIII an annulment ending his marriage to Catherine of Aragon so that he might marry Anne Boleyn, there followed a break with the Catholic Church, and the Church of England was established. All English subjects were now to be Protestants. The attempt to turn Catholics into Protestants, however, was rejected by the overwhelming majority of the population of Ireland.

This resistance came to a head in 1595 when Hugh O'Neill, the second earl of Tyrone, organized the Gaelic chiefs of Ulster, that quarter of the island now known as Northern Ireland, to rebel. The rebellion lasted eight years, during which English armies devastated Ulster. The defeated earls of Ulster were allowed to return to

King William III led his Protestant army against the deposed Catholic king, James II, in the Battle at Boyne River.

their ancestral lands under English rule, but in 1607 the legendary "Flight of the Earls" took place when they threw off British domination to sail to Europe. The British seized the earls' vast holdings and resettled English Protestants on large estates containing natural resources and farmlands. The west and central part of Northern Ireland became Ulster Plantation. There was also an influx of Presbyterian Scots brought in to manage the holdings of absentee British landlords. The native Irish were reduced to working on these estates as either migrant laborers, serfs, or sharecroppers.

The Irish Catholics of Ulster led another rebellion against the British settlers and their Scottish overseers in 1641. Thousands of Protestant civilians—men, women, and children—were slaughtered by Catholic rebels. The uprising spread throughout Ireland, and it was nine years before the English military, led by Puritan leader Oliver Cromwell, reestablished British sovereignty over the country. Cromwell then confiscated lands from Catholics throughout Ireland and turned them over to investors and army commanders who had backed the English war effort.

In 1688, James II, a Catholic who had briefly acceded to the throne of England, was deposed by King William III, known as William of Orange, a Dutch Protestant. With the help of the French, King James raised an army in Ireland, which became the main battleground for the civil war that followed. His force of 21,000 mostly untrained Irish infantry fought the deciding battle against 35,000 mercenaries on the banks of the River Boyne near Drogheda, in southern Ireland, in July 1690. King James lost and fled the country. In the wake of the war, laws were enacted barring Catholics from owning property and exercising power in Ireland. To this day, each year on July 12 in Northern Ireland, Protestants calling them-selves "Orangemen" after William of Orange parade to

Women wearing the British flag, the Union Jack, dance in the July 12, 1989, parade celebrating the victory of William of Orange.

celebrate the victory of the Boyne. These parades often provoke violence between Protestants and Catholics.

The "Popery Code"

For the next hundred years, the landowning English, called Anglo-Irish, who made up roughly 10 percent of the population of Ireland, ruled the country. They enacted and enforced the Popery Code, a series of laws that denied civil rights, property ownership, and the ability to rise economically to Catholics, who made up 75 percent of the population. The remaining 15 percent of the population, Scotch-Irish Presbyterians, were also discriminated against, but to a lesser degree.

Under the Popery Code, both Catholics and Presbyterians were forced to give money to the Church of England. They were barred from government employment and from becoming officers in the military. Catholics were barred from holding elective office, from becoming lawyers, from bearing arms, and from owning a horse worth more than five pounds. If a Catholic man died and one of his sons converted to the Church of England, the property of the deceased would all go to that son, and his Catholic siblings would receive nothing. Catholic clergy were banned from Ireland under penalty of death. In 1727 the last Popery Code law was passed. It denied Catholics the right to vote.

The Presbyterians in the nine counties of Northern Ireland fared better. In contrast to the Catholic peasants, they lived mostly middle-class lives as farmers, estate managers, or supervisors in the growing linen business. Avoiding clashes with the English, the Scotch-Irish Presbyterians established self-contained communities throughout Ulster. They did, however, clash with Northern Ireland Catholics, who regarded them as British bootlickers who persecuted them.

The Act of Union

The year 1760 marked the beginning of the Industrial Revolution, the age in which goods would be made by machine, rather than by hand. It swept over Europe and America, but bypassed most of Ireland, which was mostly farmland. The exception was Belfast and the area around it in Northern Ireland. Throughout the rest of the eighteenth century, Northern Ireland prospered and became the linen manufacturing and export center of the world.

There were side effects. Investments in Northern Ireland manufacturing compelled England to tighten its grip over the area. Industrialization brought urban problems like overcrowding, pollution, poor sanitation, and the spread of disease. These mostly affected Catholics, who by now were the poorest segment of the population. They were either hired laborers on the farms or the most menial workers in the factories. They had to compete with Scots who emigrated in large numbers to find jobs in factories and who received preferential treatment from the Protestant factory managers. Despite the growth of industry in urban areas, it was Catholics who swelled the rolls of the unemployed. By the end of the eighteenth century, while Ireland as a whole was 80 percent Catholic, in the Northern Ireland counties Catholics were a minority because of Scotch immigration.

In 1795, Ulster Protestants formed the Orange Order (so called because their forebears fought for William of Orange against the Catholic king James), and mounted a campaign of violence that forced thousands of Catholics to flee Ulster. At the same time, over the next few years, there were periodic uprisings throughout all of Ireland against British rule. Although these were suppressed, they led England's Prime Minister William Pitt to sponsor the Act of Union, calling for the merger of Ireland and England into the United Kingdom of Great Britain and Ireland with a single Parliament. The Act of Union was

The Liberator

In June 1844, sixty-eight-year-old Daniel O'Connell was jailed by the British on charges of "seditious conspiracy." O'Connell was the head of the Repeal Association, which campaigned for Ireland to secede from the United Kingdom of Great Britain and Ireland. He believed in nonviolence and that the independence struggle must be lawful.

O'Connell had joined the United Irishmen in 1797, but refused to take part in their violent uprisings. He was a leader of the unsuccessful 1804–1807 Emancipation movement to allow Catholics to serve in Parliament. Although Catholic political organizations were illegal under British law, O'Connell petitioned nationwide for Irish civil rights.

In 1823, O'Connell was a cofounder of the Catholic Association, which established a solid base of support among the Irish priesthood, lawyers, and other educated Catholics. In 1826 they organized the defeat of parliamentary candidates favored by owners of large tracts of land. Two years later, O'Connell himself was elected to Parliament. As a result of the overwhelming number of votes that O'Connell received, the law barring Catholics was repealed. He became the first Irish Catholic to serve in Parliament.

In 1837, O'Connell launched a campaign to repeal the Act of Union linking Ireland to Great Britain. In 1843 there were forty massive demonstrations throughout Ireland. When the government issued a ban against a major demonstration at Clontarf, O'Connell called it off. He had always insisted that protests be lawful and peaceful. Now he was opposed by young rebels determined to fight for Ireland's freedom.

By the time O'Connell was released from prison late in 1844, the struggle had passed him by. As the potato famine swept over the country the following year, violent actions replaced peaceful demonstrations. After his death in 1847, although O'Connell was revered as The Liberator of Ireland, his policy of nonviolence died with him.

Daniel O'Connell was the first Irish Catholic elected to serve in the British House of Commons.

This statue of Daniel O'Connell stands in Dublin as a tribute to the man who advocated a peaceful independence for Ireland.

passed in 1800. It barred Irish Catholics from becoming members of the United Kingdom Parliament.

The movement to end this prohibition was known as Emancipation. It was led by Daniel O'Connell, who believed that passive resistance exercised within the boundaries of British law could win equality for Irish Catholics. His efforts eventually led to the lifting of the ban against Irish Catholics in Parliament, and O'Connell became the first one to serve there. The successes of his nonviolent campaign for civil rights for Catholics earned him the title of The Liberator.

The Fenian Movement

In 1845 a fungus swept through Ireland and destroyed the potato crop. In the north and the south, Catholic tenant farmers were driven from the land. Famine, disease, and death swept over Ireland with two important side effects: The Catholic Church grew in membership and influence, and a violent revolutionary organization that would became the Fenian movement was born.

In 1848, as the potato famine continued, former supporters of O'Connell waged an unsuccessful war of independence. Small-scale uprisings continued throughout the 1850s and 1860s. In 1867, Fenian Catholics killed thirty innocent people in London during an unsuccessful prison break. British Prime Minister William Gladstone acknowledged that violence by the Fenians led to the 1869 repeal of the last of the Popery Code laws, which had forced Catholics to contribute to the Church of England as the official church in Ireland.

Crop failures in 1878–1879 threatened another famine, and Fenian leader Michael Davitt founded the National Land League to secure reforms for tenant farmers and to prevent their eviction by landlords. The National Land League organized communities to boy-

The Potato Famine

In Northern Ireland, as in the south, there was joy at the prospect of a bumper crop of potatoes in 1845. An article in the July 23 issue of *Freeman's Journal* reported that "the potato crop was never before so large and at the same time so abundant." There was no way to know that starvation, disease, and desolation would soon destroy that prediction.

Potatoes were the main source of food for the Irish people. One and a half acres (0.6 hectare) of land planted with potatoes could feed a family of six for a year. Pigs, cattle, and fowl also thrived on potatoes.

Sometimes called a tuber, the potato is a short, thick, fleshy underground plant stem. In Ireland potatoes were cultivated in bogs.

Planting, tending, and harvesting them was backbreaking labor. Those who performed it didn't own the land. They had to turn over a share of the crop to absentee landlords, and pay them rent as well. Others, often whole families, were migrant workers who moved from place to place harvesting the tubers as they ripened.

The economy of Ireland was dependent on potatoes. It was shattered in 1845 by the arrival of a fungus called *phytophthora infestans*, which came from the United States.

The fungus first appeared in 1842 in Maine, then moved down to East Coast potato farms, and finally spread across the country to the great plains of the Midwest. A diseased potato that crossed the Atlantic by ship carried the fungus to Europe. It spread from Germany to Belgium, France, and England, and finally, in 1845, to Ireland.

By 1846, Ireland was a devastated country. Families who worked the potato bogs were thrown out of their houses and off the land by landlords who were eager to escape financial loss by turning their properties into grazing grounds for sheep. Starvation was widespread. Families roaming the land in search of work had no sanitary facilities. People fell victim to disease, and they spread it as they moved around.

Tuberculosis reached epidemic proportions. One and a half million people died of hunger and disease between 1846 and 1851. A million more emigrated to North America.

Ireland was ruled by the British. Much of Ulster was owned by the British. When little effort was made by the British to rebuild the economy after the famine, many more Irish people left for America. Those who stayed, particularly in the north, blamed the British for the poor conditions in the country and for their own poverty. Many still do.

A Victim of Love

In 1890, the cause of Irish Home Rule fell victim to the love affair between Charles Stewart Parnell and Katherine "Kitty" O'Shea. The mother of three children, O'Shea was the wife of Captain William O'Shea, a member of the British Parliament. On November 17, Captain O'Shea was granted a divorce on grounds of adultery after naming Parnell as his wife's lover.

Charles Parnell was born into an Anglo-Irish Protestant landowning family in County Wicklow, Ireland, on June 27, 1846. As a youth he developed sympathy for the down-trodden Irish peasants. Despite his privileged status, he grew up to champion their cause. At the age of twenty-nine, he was elected to the British Parliament as an advocate of Home Rule for Ireland. During the next four years, Parnell became president of both the Home Rule Confederation and the Irish Land League.

He gained wide support among Irish Catholics by strongly supporting rights for tenant farmers. He organized protests in Ireland and persuaded thirty-six Irish members of Parliament to block discussion until Irish demands were heard. In October 1881, he was jailed for making rabble-rousing speeches. Captain O'Shea, although aware of Parnell's affair with his wife, negotiated his release.

In 1882, Parnell's leadership was tested when two British officials were assassinated in Dublin. Revulsion against terrorism split the Irish movement. Parnell arbitrated between those for violent action and those against it. He succeeded in restoring unity in support of Home Rule. Then, in 1887, *The Times* of London published a letter, allegedly written by Parnell, condoning the murders.

Charles Parnell was a member of the British Parliament and advocated Irish Home Rule and Irish independence from Britain.

His denial was confirmed two years later when the letter's forger confessed before killing himself. Parnell was restored as a hero to the Irish people.

The following year political differences led Captain O'Shea to make public the affair between his wife and Parnell. As a result, the Irish-Catholic bishops denounced Parnell. The Irish Party in Parliament removed him as its leader. His political career was over. Seven months after the divorce, in June 1891, Parnell and Kitty O'Shea were married. Four months later, at the age of forty-five, Charles Stewart Parnell died following a long illness.

cott, to refuse to sell goods or provide labor to, landlords who were guilty of abuses. The cause of the Land League was championed by Charles Stewart Parnell, a Protestant who gained the allegiance of Catholics by fighting for home rule for Ireland in Parliament. Parnell was responsible for Parliament passing the Land Act of 1881, which ensured fair rents for tenant farmers, protection against evictions, and the right of a tenant to sell his farm lease to another tenant. For 270 years, Irish farmers had been agitating for these rights, and now, thanks to Parnell and Davitt, they had them.

The reforms were more important to Catholics in the south than to those in Northern Ireland. By the end of the nineteenth century, six of the nine counties of Northern Ireland were becoming increasingly industrialized. Belfast had become a major shipbuilding center, and a major seaport as well. By now, Catholics were barely a third of the population. More and more of them were working in factories rather than on the land. As all of Ireland struggled against the poverty perpetuated by British rule, Ulster prospered because of the availability of cheap Catholic labor subject to ongoing Protestant discrimination. Northern Ireland had become too rich a prize for the English to surrender. It would be the major Irish battleground of the twentieth century.

Chapter 2

The Partition of Ireland

The twentieth century began with the battle over Home Rule for Ireland. With a bloc of Irish members of Parliament holding the balance of power between the two major British parties, a promise was extracted from Prime Minister Herbert H. Asquith to back a Home Rule bill. In opposition to it, thousands of Northern Ireland Protestants led by Sir Edward Carson signed the Ulster Covenant, vowing resistance to being separated from Protestant England and coming under the domination of Catholic Ireland.

In 1912, Carson announced that if Home Rule passed for Ireland, a separate government would be formed in Northern Ireland. In effect, Northern Ireland would declare itself independent of Ireland. At first the Ulster Unionists, as they called themselves, opposed Home Rule for all of Ireland. Later they adopted a fall-

Opposite:
Edward Carson and many other Protestants spoke out against the Catholics who wanted Home Rule for Ireland.

back demand that Ulster be excluded from Irish Home Rule if it was passed by Parliament.

The Unionists organized the Ulster Volunteer Force and armed it to fight for separation from Catholic Ireland. There was widespread sympathy among Protestant officers in the British army. The officers in one cavalry brigade announced that they would resign if ordered to enforce Home Rule in Ulster. In 1913 the Irish Volunteers were organized in Dublin to resist the Ulster Volunteers. Both forces began stockpiling arms and ammunition.

Ireland was on the verge of civil war in 1914 when Great Britain was plunged into World War I. The possibility of Irish civil war posed a major threat to the British war effort. To prevent an Irish rebellion, the British Parliament at long last passed Home Rule legislation. To pacify the Ulster Unionists, the bill called for a separate vote to determine the fate of the counties of Northern Ireland. It also postponed implementation of Home Rule until the end of World War I.

The Rising Tide

Most of the Irish people supported England in the war against Germany. More than 150,000 Irishmen enlisted in the British army. While they were fighting, and often dying in the trenches, a militant minority saw things differently. The Irish Republican Brotherhood (IRB), a Fenian group, believing that the Home Rule legislation was a stalling maneuver by the English, decided that the time had come to rebel. An IRB representative was smuggled into Germany to seek military assistance, but his mission was a failure.

Nevertheless, Easter week 1916 brought Irish rebellion against English rule. Mostly, the fighting was confined to Dublin. The uprising was quickly put down by

the British, and the leaders were executed. Martial law and brutal military actions against the Irish populace followed. British ruthlessness added fuel to the myth of the heroic Easter Rising. As memory grew into legend, it inspired rebellion among the youth of Ireland, and particularly the persecuted Catholic youth of Northern Ireland.

The English incorrectly blamed the Easter rebellion on Sinn Fein, an organization formed in 1905 by Arthur Griffith. Sinn Fein, however, was a nonviolent group advocating Irish independence through political means,

The wreck of a burned-out car in front of ruined buildings after the Easter Rising in Dublin, 1916

The Easter Rising

By 1916, a militant minority in Ireland opposed siding with the British in World War I. Fifteen thousand anti-British troops led by Eoin MacNeill of the Gaelic League had left the British army. The Irish Republican Brotherhood (IRB), believing that the Home Rule legislation was a stalling maneuver by the English, decided that the time had come to rebel. They wanted MacNeill's troops to spearhead the uprising. MacNeill, fearing failure, was against taking action.

IRB leader Padraig Pearse believed that "blood sacrifice" creating martyrs to inspire future rebellions would eventually free Ireland. He persuaded the IRB leadership to order the Irish Volunteers to take military action. MacNeill immediately revoked the order. There followed a series of conflicting commands, which led to great confusion.

The rebellion, meant to start on Easter Sunday, was delayed until Easter Monday, April 24, 1916. The intended nationwide uprising became an action confined to Dublin and involved only 1,600 rebels. The rebels seized a number of public buildings, made the Dublin General Post Office their command post, and proclaimed the Irish Republic.

Initially, British troops ran from the rebels. Then they regrouped and brought up reinforcements. The fighting lasted five days. The British suffered more than 500 casualties, including 112 dead. On April 29 the rebels surrendered.

At first, the action was not popular with the citizens of Dublin. They called the rebels hotheads and jeered at them as the British marched them off to jail. Irish newspapers were horrified by the violence and blamed the rebels for it.

Padraig Pearse was an Irish writer, educator, and politician who led the Easter Rising in 1916 and was executed by the British.

These attitudes changed when the British held short, secret trials, and then executed fifteen of the rebels. Martial law followed and resulted in the shooting of many unarmed Irish civilians by British troops. The last straw was a threat to draft young Irishmen into the British army.

Within six weeks of the Easter rebellion, pictures of the executed rebels draped in black hung in every pub. Ballads were sung in praise of them. Poems were written glorifying them as "martyred prisoners of war" murdered by the British. Most cherished among the dead martyrs was Padraig Pearse.

"DAILY EXPRESS." FREE INSURANCE. £1,000 at death. £1 10s. a week while disabled. £500 for loss of eye or limb. And other benefits. SEE PAGE 6.

Daily Express

Late War EDITION

FREE ADVERTISEMENTS FOR DISABLED SOLDIERS AND SAILORS. SEE PAGE SIX.

NO. 5,008. LONDON, WEDNESDAY, APRIL 26, 1916. ONE HALFPENNY.

Secret Session—Dublin Revolt—Naval Raid on England.

CRAZY REBELLION IN IRELAND.

ARMED SINN FEINERS SEIZE POST OFFICE AND STREETS IN DUBLIN.

CITY ISOLATED.

11 KILLED AND 17 WOUNDED IN THE FIGHTING.

A grave rebellion in Dublin has followed the attempt by a German vessel to land arms and ammunition in Ireland and the arrest of Sir Roger Casement, the renegade ex-Consul. Official news available last night showed that there were two centres of the rebellion, which was organised by Sinn Feiners, as follows :—

North of the River: The Post Office, Sackville-street, Abbey-street, and the Quays.

South of the River: St. Stephen's Green.

Telegraph and telephone wires had been cut.

Troops from the Curragh have arrived, and have the situation well in hand.

The casualties reported number eleven or twelve killed and seventeen or nineteen wounded, as follows :—

Officers killed, three; wounded, four or five.

Soldiers killed, four or five; wounded, seven or eight.

Policemen killed, two.

Loyal volunteers killed, two; wounded, six.

The casualties among the rebels are not known.

LIMITED TO DUBLIN.

The following official statement was issued last evening by the Chief Secretary for Ireland :—

At noon yesterday serious disturbances broke out in **DUBLIN.** A large body of men identified with the Sinn Feiners, mostly armed, occupied **STEPHEN'S GREEN** and took possession forcibly of the **POST OFFICE,** where they cut the telegraphic and telephonic wires.

Houses were also occupied in **STEPHEN'S GREEN, SACKVILLE STREET, ABBEY STREET,** and along the **QUAYS.**

In the course of the day soldiers arrived from the **CURRAGH,** and the situation is now well in hand.

So far as is known here—

Three military officers, four or five soldiers, two loyal volunteers, and two policemen have been killed, and

Four or five military officers, seven or eight soldiers, and six loyal volunteers wounded.

No exact information has been received of casualties on the side of the Sinn Feiners.

Reports received from **CORK, LIMERICK, ENNIS, TRALEE,** and both Ridings of **TIPPERARY** show that no disturbances of any kind have occurred in these localities.

QUESTIONS IN PARLIAMENT.

The first news of the rebellion was announced in the House of Commons yesterday by Mr. Birrell, in reply to a question by Colonel James Craig (U., Down, E.), who asked if the Chief Secretary for Ireland was prepared to make a statement regarding the situation in the Irish capital.

MR. BIRRELL said:

At noon yesterday grave disturbances broke out in Dublin. The Post Office was forcibly taken possession of,

SIR R. CASEMENT'S TRIAL.

BROUGHT TO LONDON IN MILITARY CUSTODY.

HIS ACTS IN GERMANY.

The following official statement in connection with the arrest of Sir Roger Casement was issued yesterday :—

Sir Roger Casement, whose arrest in connection with the abortive attempt to land arms in Ireland from a German vessel was announced yesterday, was brought to London on Sunday morning.

He was met at Euston by officers from Scotland-yard, and is now detained in military custody.

It is understood that evidence as to his proceedings in Germany since the outbreak of war will be produced at his trial.

In the House of Commons yesterday Mr. Pemberton Billing put the following question to the Prime Minister:—

"Is it a fact that Sir Roger Casement has been brought to London, and can the Prime Minister give the House and the nation an assurance that this traitor will be shot forthwith?" (Loud laughter and cheers.)

Mr. Asquith replied: "I do not think that is a question that ought to be put to me at present." (Cheers.)

The law of high treason and its penalties are explained on Page 4.

IRELAND'S RULERS.

The head of the Executive Government of Ireland at Dublin Castle is Lord Wimborne, who succeeded the Earl of Aberdeen as Lord Lieutenant last year. He is in his forty-fourth year, and fought with the Yeomanry in South Africa.

Under the Lord Lieutenant the most important official at Dublin Castle is Lieut.-Colonel Sir Matthew Nathan, who became Permanent Under-Secretary in October 1914, in succession to Sir James Dougherty.

He is fifty-four years of age, and has had a distinguished career both in the military and colonial services. He was successively Governor of the Gold Coast, Hongkong, and Natal. For two years he was Secretary to the Post Office, and for the two years preceding his present employment he was Chairman of the Board of Inland Revenue.

STREET MAP OF DUBLIN.

DOWNING-STREET CONFERENCE.

Mr. Asquith returned to Downing-street early yesterday morning, and among his first visitors was Mr. Birrell, Secretary for Ireland, who arrived shortly after eleven o'clock, accompanied by Mr. Samuel, the Home Secretary.

THE SECRET SESSION.

CABINET PLANS TO SECURE 200,000 MORE MEN.

AID FOR THE MARRIED

GRANTS TO BE MADE UP TO £104 A YEAR.

Parliament sat in secret yesterday, and both Houses were informed of the Government's recruiting proposals and plans for the financial relief of married men called to the colours. The secret session will be continued to-day.

Compulsion for all is to be enforced unless:—

50,000 unattested married men are recruited before May 27.

15,000 a week are obtained after that date.

200,000 are obtained in all.

Immediate expedients to be adopted are the retention of time-expired men with the colours, the transfer of Territorials to ordinary battalions, the compulsory enlistment of youths as they reach the age of eighteen, and the compulsion of exempted men immediately after their exemptions are cancelled.

Financial relief will be extended to all men who enlisted since August 4, 1914. It will be paid in respect of rent, taxes, rates, insurance premiums, mortgage interest, payments in instalments in virtue of contracts, and school fees, but not in respect of ordinary debts.

Not more than £104 per annum will be granted. Applications for relief will be considered locally by commissioners.

OFFICIAL REPORT.

At a very late hour—too late for it to be included in all the editions of the newspapers—the following official report of the proceedings was issued :—

The Prime Minister, in moving the adjournment of the House, gave particulars of the expansion of the Army from the first days of the war up to the present time, and of the total military effort of the Empire, including the contributions from the self-governing Dominions, and from India.

He reviewed the inquiries conducted by the Government in order to examine all considerations relevant to the recruiting problem, including the demands made on our supply of labour in providing for the needs of the Navy, the mercantile marine, ports, munitions, and other essential national services. The bearing of finance on the question of recruiting, and, in particular, of the financial assistance rendered to our allies, was then explained. From these inquiries were deduced the number of men that could be safely spared from industry for military purposes during the present year, and the anticipated effect of calling up these numbers at the rate proposed was explained.

NOT ENOUGH MEN.

The results of recruiting, more particularly since August last, when registration was carried out, were reviewed. It was shown that the results obtained up to

AIR ATTACKS BY THE BRITISH.

ENEMY AERODROME IN BELGIUM BOMBED.

GOOD RESULTS.

ADMIRALTY, Wednesday, 12.10 a.m.

On the morning of the 23rd inst., in spite of most inclement weather, a bombing attack was carried out by naval aeroplanes upon the enemy aerodrome at Mariakerke. The machines were heavily fired on, but succeeded in returning safely. As far as could be observed, good results were obtained. One of our fighting machines attacked an enemy aeroplane, and drove it down. The hostile machine, when last seen, was close to the ground and out of control.

On the morning of the 24th inst. another attack was carried out on the same objective, in cooperation with our Belgian allies, and a large number of bombs were dropped. Heavy fire was encountered by all machines, but there were no British casualties. The result obtained appeared to have been very good.

During the course of the same day (24th inst.) a British aeroplane attacked an enemy seaplane about five miles off Zeebrugge. The enemy pilot was killed, and the machine dropped, the enemy observer falling out while the machine was still at a height of 3,000 feet. The hostile seaplane crashed into the sea and sank.

Mariakerke is a village on the coast of Belgium two miles west of Ostend.

29 COMBATS IN THE AIR.

British Official.

FROM SIR DOUGLAS HAIG.

GENERAL HEADQUARTERS, Tuesday, 10.15 p.m.

Yesterday there was considerable aerial activity. Twenty-nine combats took place. One of our reconnaissances was persistently attacked. All the attacks were driven off, and two hostile machines were seen to fall to the ground in the German lines. All our machines returned safely.

Enemy sprang mines near Fricourt and Souchez without inflicting any casualties. We bombarded enemy's positions just north of the Somme. Some artillery activity between Souchez and the La Bassée Canal, also in the Armentières sector, where our guns shelled the railway stations of Comines and Warneton.

LIQUID FIRE ATTACK.

FRESH GERMAN FAILURE AT THE DEAD MAN.

French Official.

PARIS, Tuesday, April 25.

The following communiqué was issued this afternoon:—

West of the Meuse towards the end of the day yesterday, after a violent bombardment, the Germans made several attacks on our new positions in the region of the Dead Man. The two first attempts having completely failed, the enemy launched a final attack, supported by copious use of flaming liquid. Swept by our curtain and infantry fire, the Germans were forced to return to their lines

COMBINED NAVAL AND AIR RAID.

LOWESTOFT BOMBARDED BY GERMAN BATTLE-CRUISERS.

ENEMY'S FLIGHT AFTER ACTION WITH LIGHT SQUADRON.

A raid on Lowestoft by the German battle cruiser squadron took place at 4.30 yesterday morning—a few hours after the Zeppelin raid on the eastern counties, which was reported in yesterday's "Daily Express." The two raids were probably not unconnected. It is more than likely that the Zeppelins were engaged in a reconnoitring expedition on behalf of the warships.

The official statements on the two raids are as follows :—

THE NAVAL RAID.

ADMIRALTY, Tuesday, 1.40 p.m.

About 4.30 this morning the German battle cruiser squadron, accompanied by light cruisers and destroyers, appeared off Lowestoft. The local naval forces engaged it and in about twenty minutes it returned to Germany, chased by our light cruisers and destroyers.

On shore, two men, one woman, and a child were killed. The material damage seems to have been insignificant.

So far as is known at present, two British light cruisers and a destroyer were hit, but none was sunk.

SEAPLANES ATTACK SUBMARINES.

ADMIRALTY, Wednesday Morning.

During the operations against the German battle cruiser squadron which appeared off the east coast on the morning of the 25th inst., two Zeppelins were pursued by naval land machines over sixty miles out to sea. Bombs and darts were dropped, but apparently without serious effect. An aeroplane and a seaplane attacked the German ships off Lowestoft, dropping heavy bombs. Four enemy submarines were also attacked by bombs. One seaplane came under heavy fire from the hostile fleet, but the pilot, although seriously wounded, succeeded in bringing his machine safely back to land.

It is regretted that one pilot is reported missing. He ascended during the course of the Zeppelin raid earlier in the morning and appears from reports to have attacked a Zeppelin off Lowestoft at about 1.5 a.m. He has not been heard of since.

THE AIR RAID.

WAR OFFICE, Tuesday, 3 p.m.

Last night's air raid over the Norfolk and Suffolk coasts appears to have been carried out by four or five Zeppelins, only two of which made any serious attempt to penetrate inland.

About seventy bombs appear to have been dropped. One man is reported seriously injured.

No further details as to casualties are yet available.

AIR AND SEA RAID ON ZEEBRUGGE.

GERMAN DESTROYERS HIT AND DRIVEN INTO PORT.

AMSTERDAM, Tuesday, April 25.

A message received here from Flushing states that yesterday morning several

FOURTEEN BOMBS ON ONE TOWN.

LONDON STOCKBROKER INJURED.

A Zeppelin passed over an east-coast town at 12.45 a.m. yesterday, and dropped fourteen bombs, two incendiary

Front page of the *Daily Express* after the Easter Rising with headlines reading "Crazy Rebellion in Ireland"

A mural commemorating Easter week 1916, decorates the side of a Catholic apartment building in Belfast, Northern Ireland.

not military action. Since the violence advocated by other rebels revolted many Catholics, Sinn Fein gained popularity with the Irish people. In 1918 a majority of Sinn Fein members were elected to Parliament, but refused to serve. Instead, they constituted themselves the legislature of the revolutionary Republic of Ireland, passed a Declaration of Independence from Great Britain, and demanded that English troops leave all of Ireland, including Ulster. Eamon De Valera was elected president of the new republic.

Anticipating that the British army would move to suppress the new republic, the Irish legislature abandoned nonviolence and authorized a militia to defend it. This was the birth of the Irish Republican Army (IRA). Over the next two years there was wide support for the IRA in Ireland as they waged guerrilla warfare against the British.

Large numbers of Irish county and municipal police resigned to join the IRA. They were replaced by English recruits known by their uniforms as Black-and-Tans. There were sporadic incidents of violence in Northern Ireland, but for the most part the civil war was fought in the rest of the country. In 1920 the British government passed the Government of Ireland Act dividing the nation into two self-governing areas—Northern Ireland and Southern Ireland. A year later parliamentarian Michael Collins signed a treaty making the Irish Free State a dominion of Great Britain. Under the terms of the treaty, the six wealthiest counties of Northern Ireland—Antrim, Armagh, Down, Fermanagh, Londonderry, and Tyrone—remained under direct British rule. The population of these counties was roughly one-third Catholic and two-thirds Protestant.

Civil War

When the Irish legislature approved the treaty, Eamon De Valera resigned as president. He became a political leader of the Irish Republican forces opposed to the treaty. As positions hardened, a bloody civil war between pro-partition and anti-partition Irish forces broke out. With help from the English, the new Irish government under Michael Collins was particularly brutal in putting down the anti-partition rebels. Now Catholics were killing Catholics.

Hero or Traitor?

Michael Collins survived the Easter Rising to become a legendary Irish hero. He was also the statesman who abandoned Northern Ireland to the British and incited civil war. Once hailed as a hero, he was assassinated as a traitor.

Born in County Cork in 1890, Collins went to London at the age of sixteen. He was a British civil servant until 1916 when he returned to Dublin to fight in support of the rebels. He was arrested and imprisoned from April through December 1916.

In 1918, Collins was elected to the Irish parliament, which ratified the republic proclaimed by the 1916 rebels. With elected President Eamon De Valera in prison, Collins virtually ran the outlaw republic. In 1919, Collins engineered De Valera's escape from jail and flight from the country.

For the next two years, Collins served as director of intelligence of the Irish army in its struggle against the British. They regarded him as chief planner of the revolution. A reward of 10,000 pounds was offered by the British for his capture dead or alive.

After a 1921 truce was arranged with the British, DeValera returned, and Collins went to London to negotiate a treaty. On December 6, 1921, Collins agreed to terms that he believed were "the best that could be obtained for Ireland." The treaty left six counties of Northern Ireland under British rule. De Valera and other Irish leaders refused to accept it. Nevertheless, a majority of the Irish parliament agreed to it.

Civil war followed. Collins assumed command of the Irish Free State army. He borrowed artillery from the British to bombard the Dublin headquarters of the anti-treaty rebels. Seventy-seven rebels were executed. Collins's forces burned down homes and jailed 11,000 rebel sympathizers.

When Arthur Griffith, the president of the Irish Free State, died in 1922, Collins became head of the government. Ten days later, on August 22, Michael Collins was ambushed and killed. His assassination was rumored to have been ordered by Eamon De Valera, from his jail cell in the Irish Free State.

Future Irish president Michael Collins wearing the Irish Volunteers
uniform around the time of the Easter Rising in 1916

The Irish delegation on the day Michael Collins signed the treaty (from left): Arthur Griffith, Eamonn Duggan, Erskine Childers, Michael Collins, George Gavan Duffy, Robert Barton, and John Chartres

In Belfast, pro-partition Protestants responded by slaughtering Catholics and burning down their homes. On June 22, 1922, in London, Field Marshal Sir Henry Wilson, recently named military adviser to the government of Northern Ireland, was assassinated. In Dublin, anti-partition Republican forces surrendered. Finally, in May 1923, on Eamon De Valera's recommendation, the armed resistance ended.

The Republican Party of De Valera won 44 seats out of 128 in the new Irish legislature—called the Dail—in August 1923. However, the Republicans refused to take the oath of loyalty to the British crown required of dominion legislators, and so they could not serve in the

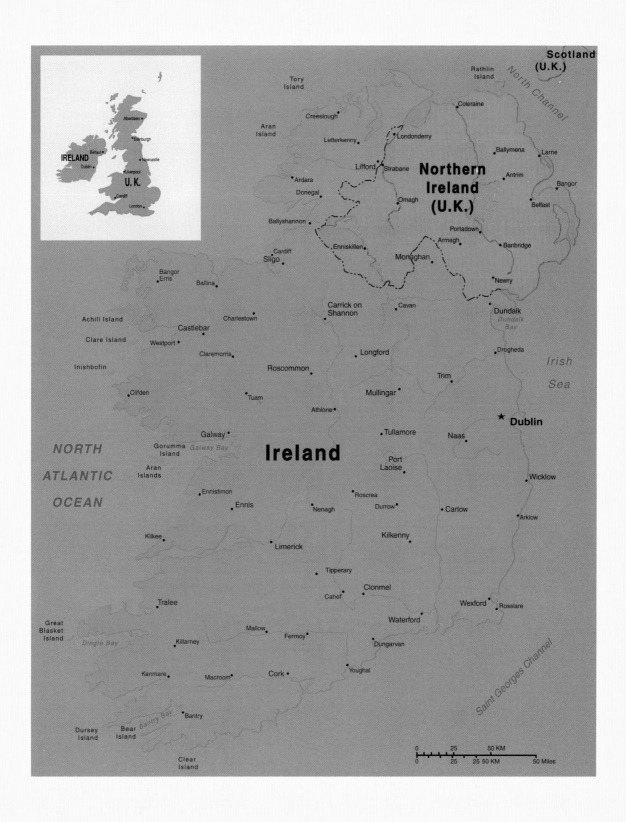

Dail. They continued to refuse during the next four years, but finally, in 1927, under protest, they made the pledge. By 1932 they were able to form a government under De Valera, which would remain in power over most of the next four decades.

An Uneasy Truce

On June 22, 1921, the British dominion of Northern Ireland set up its own parliament with Sir James Craig as prime minister. He was a member of the Unionist Party, which, because it represented majority Protestant opinion, was the only effective political party in Northern Ireland. The key decision makers among the Unionists were all members of the Orange Order. In effect, the Catholic minority in Northern Ireland would have little or no political representation for decades to come.

Throughout the 1920s there were periodic depressions in Ulster. Because of changes in fashions in many countries, there was a decline in the market for linen. Shipbuilding fell off. Women workers, and then men, lost their jobs. Wages were reduced. The lowest class of workers was the Catholics, and they were hardest hit by waves of unemployment. In 1929, following the stock market crash in the United States, the two large Belfast shipyards, which were the city's main employers, began to lay off skilled workers in large numbers. Following the firings, Protestants banded together with Catholics to demand relief for the unemployed. They split apart again, however, when the 1932 election of De Valera as president of Ireland raised the specter of the Free State marshaling the IRA to reclaim Ulster.

In November 1932, in the midst of the depression, a major landowner and Unionist member of the Northern Ireland Parliament, Sir Basil Brooke, recommended that

The People's Choice

Eamon De Valera was born in New York City in 1882. His father was a Spanish artist who died when Eamon was an infant. The child was sent back to County Limerick, Ireland, to be raised in near poverty by his mother's family.

A determined student, he worked hard to put himself through the Royal University. In 1913 he joined the Irish Volunteers to fight for Home Rule. In the 1916 Easter Rising, he was the last commander to surrender. The British sentenced him to be executed. Because he was technically an American citizen, the sentence was not carried out.

In 1919 the imprisoned De Valera was elected president of the Sinn Fein party. A year later, he escaped from prison. He fled to the United States to raise funds for Sinn Fein. He returned to Ireland when a truce with the British was declared, and assigned Michael Collins to negotiate a treaty.

When the Irish parliament accepted the Collins treaty leaving six Northern counties under British rule, De Valera joined the armed opposition. He was jailed, then released after the civil war.

He organized a political party and in 1927 signed a loyalty pledge to the British crown, calling it "an empty political formula." Once he and his supporters were in parliament, however, they campaigned to end the oath.

In 1932, De Valera was named prime minister by a coalition government and began severing Ireland's ties with Great Britain. When land taxes were withheld, Britain retaliated with economic sanctions. De Valera persuaded the Irish that the resulting hardships were worthwhile.

De Valera declared the Irish Free State a sovereign nation—the Republic of Ireland—rather than a British dominion in 1937. When World War II broke out in 1939, he proclaimed Ireland neutral. He was credited with keeping Ireland free of the burdens of war while reaping the benefits of wartime prosperity.

For twenty-one of the years between 1932 and 1959, De Valera was prime minister of Ireland. He was president from 1959 through 1973. In 1975, he died. Northern Ireland Catholics lost their foremost champion against British rule.

Ulster loyalists "employ Protestant lads and lassies," rather than "disloyal" Catholics. Prime Minister Craig agreed, declaring that "we are a Protestant Parliament and a Protestant State." Tensions mounted, and in 1935 when there were celebrations to mark the jubilee of King George V of England (twenty-five years as monarch), Protestants and Catholics clashed in Belfast. Because of the clashes, the annual Twelfth of July parade by Orangemen to celebrate the victory of the Boyne was banned. When the Orange Order reacted with fury, the ban was lifted. The parade proceeded, and when it reached Catholic areas in the north of the city, serious rioting broke out. It lasted for days. Catholics were beaten and murdered, and their homes were burned down. When it was over, thirteen people were dead and three hundred were left homeless.

An extended period of relative calm followed. It was marred by IRA raids—some from the south, most originating in the north—targeting British soldiers. As part of Great Britain, Northern Ireland fought against the Germans in World War II, and some of the IRA actions may have been sponsored and financed by Germany.

Sinn Fein activities had spread from the Free State to both Northern Ireland and the United States, where money was regularly raised to further the cause of a united Ireland. The ties between Sinn Fein and the IRA became stronger, and much of this money was undoubtedly used to arm the IRA. By the end of World War II, it was hard to tell whether Sinn Fein was the political wing of the IRA in Northern Ireland, or the IRA was the military force of Sinn Fein.

Despite sporadic IRA activity and Orange responses, an uneasy truce prevailed between Catholics and Protestants throughout World War II. The war had brought relative prosperity to the factories and shipbuilding facilities of Northern Ireland, and with economic pressures lifted, and full employment, religious rivalries were on the back burner. With the new anti-British Republic of Ireland neutral in the war, and Ulster actively participating alongside England, the ties between Northern Ireland and the British Empire became stronger than ever. Although Catholics remained second-class citizens, peace prevailed for the most part until the 1960s. That was when young Catholics, inspired by the struggle for civil rights in the United States, began their fight to secure equality for their own people in Northern Ireland.

Chapter 3

From "Bloody Sunday" to Good Friday

In the late 1960s the Catholics of Northern Ireland were truly second-class citizens. Many Catholics could not vote because they did not own property, as was required by law. They were discriminated against in employment, housing, and education, and persecuted by their neighbors and by the Royal Ulster Constabulary (RUC), the national police force. It had been that way for Catholics since the 1920s when Ulster was partitioned from the Irish Free State, which occupied the major part of the island of Ireland.

The Catholic civil-rights movement was meant to be nonviolent. From the first, however, it met with violence. In 1968 peaceful marchers were attacked by the RUC. In 1969 students marching from Belfast to Derry were set upon by militant Orangemen. Through the early 1970s the violence mounted, culminating in Bloody Sunday.

Opposite:
British troops in Belfast armed with automatic rifles and bayonets in August 1969

At that time Northern Ireland, although a British territory, had "home rule" by a Protestant-controlled parliament. Bloody Sunday changed that. The British abolished the parliament and established direct control of the government backed up by an occupying army. They also instituted prohibitions against anti-Catholic discrimination in housing, employment, and education.

Bloody Sunday had another effect. It encouraged militants known as Provos within the IRA to take action. To the Provos, the British were an enemy to be driven out of Northern Ireland by any means necessary. The aim was to unite Northern Ireland with the Irish Free State. This threatened Protestants—most of whom were wary of Orange militancy and wanted nothing so much as peace—with becoming a minority in a nation subject to Catholic doctrine.

On Bloody Sunday, many protestors in Derry were arrested by British soldiers and searched at gunpoint. Thirteen were killed.

The Provos

In the early 1970s demonstrations for Catholic civil rights in Northern Ireland were put down violently by the 93 percent Protestant Royal Ulster Constabulary (RUC), and by blatantly anti-Catholic British troops. At this time the IRA had halted military action to agitate for social reforms. Graffiti appeared in Catholic neighborhoods declaring "IRA=I Ran Away." This inspired the Provisional IRA (known as Provos) to split off from the main organization in order to launch a campaign of terror and violence against Protestants.

Following the murder of Catholic protesters by British troops on Bloody Sunday in 1972, Provo violence escalated, forcing the British to abolish the Protestant controlled "home rule" Parliament. The British army then ruled Northern Ireland. This led to more than twenty years of violence by the Provos, and retribution by Protestant paramilitary forces.

In 1994 the Provos ceased operations to engage in peace talks. When they stalled in 1996, Provos set off a bomb in London, killing two civilians. Since then, Provo commitment to the peace process has been an on-again, off-again question.

A Catholic in Belfast, Northern Ireland, throws a gas bomb
at a British armored car in this 1981 photograph.

Overcoming "The Troubles"

Throughout the 1970s and 1980s, there was mounting violence between the IRA and Protestant paramilitary groups with ties to the Orange Order. The rejuvenated IRA built pride among Catholics who had been mostly passive under Protestant domination since the 1920s. As a result there was a Catholic boycott of a 1973 British-sponsored vote to determine if Northern Ireland should have independence or remain part of Great Britain. With only Protestants voting, the result was overwhelmingly in favor of staying within the United Kingdom.

The British tried to back away from ruling Northern Ireland by setting up a provisional local government with an eleven-member executive council that included four Catholics. When both IRA and Orange violence intensified, however, a general strike paralyzed Northern

The Loyal Orange Order

On July 12, 1998, Richard, Mark, and Jason Quinn, eleven, nine, and seven years old, were burned alive in their home in County Atrim. They were Catholic victims of a gasoline bomb thrown during a clash between the Loyal Orange Order and the Royal Ulster Constabulary (RUC). At issue was an Orange parade through a Catholic neighborhood.

The Loyal Orange Order is a worldwide Irish society pledged to defend Protestant interests. Traditionally, Northern Ireland members have been loyal to the British crown as a barrier against Catholic challenges to Protestant power.

Every year on July 12, they celebrate the victory of William of Orange over the Catholic king James II at the Battle of the Boyne in 1690 with a parade. More often than not, parades have erupted into violence against Catholics.

Although the Orange Order is the largest Protestant organization in Northern Ireland, its militancy has cost it support among moderate Protestants. Once a major force against sharing political power with Catholics, the Orange Order is viewed today as a weakened roadblock to peace.

Ireland, and the British resumed direct rule. They again tried to set up an Irish assembly to take over the government in 1982, but bombings and shootings by both sides continued. Finally, in 1985, Britain and the Republic of Ireland signed an agreement giving the Republic a voice in the affairs of Northern Ireland. Catholics saw hope in this. Protestants feared it would open the way to Catholic rule.

Negotiations aimed at returning Northern Ireland to local rule began in the 1990s, but they broke down in 1992. The next year Great Britain and the Republic of Ireland issued the Downing Street Declaration, inviting Sinn Fein, the political wing of the IRA, to renounce violence and join the peace talks. On August 31, 1994, the IRA announced a "complete cessation of military operations." Talks began between Sinn Fein and the British.

The truce lasted seventeen months, but little progress was made. The IRA grew increasingly distrustful of British intentions. To force their hand, on February 9, 1996, the IRA announced that the cease-fire was over. That same day they set off a huge bomb in the London financial district, killing two. More than a hundred people were injured, eight seriously. Nine days later the IRA exploded a bomb on a London bus, killing one person and injuring eight. World opinion, which had applauded the IRA truce, now turned against what was widely regarded as barbarous terrorism.

Talks were broken off by the Ulster Unionist Party, which had long represented the Protestant majority in politics. The stalemate was dealt with slowly by the intervention of an international panel headed by former U. S. Senator George Mitchell. He persuaded the British to drop their insistence that the IRA disarm before entering new negotiations. After the IRA instituted another cease-fire in July 1997, Mitchell's six principles of nonviolence were agreed to, and both Sinn Fein and the Ulster Unionists rejoined the peace talks.

(From left:) Sinn Fein leader Gerry Adams, Irish Prime Minister Albert Reynolds, and Social Democratic and Labour Party leader John Hume after a negotiation session in September 1994

In 1998 an agreement was reached giving Catholics a strong voice in a new government while granting Protestant demands that Northern Ireland remain a part of Great Britain. Known as the Good Friday Agreement, it was overwhelmingly approved by voters in the north and in the Irish Republic in May 1998. Backers of the Good Friday Agreement were elected to a majority of the seats in the new Northern Ireland Assembly.

Praising the Good Friday Agreement, U.S. president Bill Clinton said that it "reflected more than the common humanity that unites the people of Northern Ireland, no matter their faith. It reflected their self-

The Peace Movement

A spontaneous and nonpolitical peace movement involving tens of thousands of Catholics and Protestants sprang up in Northern Ireland in 1976. It followed the killing of the three children of Anne Corrigan by the runaway car of a terrorist gang. The children's aunt Mairead Corrigan, joined by Betty Williams and journalist Ciaran McKeown, organized peace marches through Belfast and other trouble spots. The movement developed a Peace Assembly and a platform that was extremely critical of the political establishment, as well as of militant groups on both sides. Partly because of this, as the violence mounted, support for the peace movement declined. Although Mairead Corrigan and Betty Williams were awarded the Nobel Peace Prize, by 1980 the movement was no longer an influence on events in Northern Ireland.

Betty Williams (left) and Mairead Corrigan (right) wave telegrams of support
from Protestants and Catholics during a "Women for Peace" rally in August 1976.

A man rests early on a July morning in 1996 after a night of rioting in a Belfast neighborhood.

interest—their heartfelt conviction that the sacrifices and compromises required for peace would be far easier to bear than the burden of more violence and bloodshed." That was the hope and the promise, but it was yet to be fulfilled.

Chapter 4

A Long, Hard Road

The Good Friday Agreement of 1998 was regarded as an important step in the struggle for Catholic civil rights in Northern Ireland. To Protestants it brought the prospect of peace. People of goodwill on both sides had high hopes for the new talks between the recently elected first minister of Northern Ireland David Trimble, who was also head of the Protestant majority Ulster Unionist Party; John Hume, leader of the moderate Catholic Social Democratic and Labour Party, and Gerry Adams, president of Sinn Fein. These hopes were dealt a blow by the most tragic bloodbath in the recent history of Northern Ireland, the bombing of Omagh on August 15, 1998.

Slaughter at Omagh

Omagh is a small city in County Tyrone in the center of Northern Ireland. It has a population of roughly 8,200

Opposite:
Hundreds of mourners came to pay their respects at the funeral of a mother and daughter who were killed in the Omagh bombing on August 15, 1998.

Two firemen work to hose down one of the buildings in the shopping district of Omagh, Northern Ireland, where debris littered the street after the bombing on August 15, 1998.

people. Most of the residents are Catholic, and a council chairman of Sinn Fein lives there. There had always been strong support for Sinn Fein in Omagh, and that summer there was strong support for Sinn Fein's role in the Good Friday Agreement peace talks.

The talks were opposed by an ultramilitant group that had broken off from the Provisional IRA. Calling themselves the "Real IRA," they had been setting off bombs in Northern Ireland since Easter without actually killing anybody. The bomb they set off in Omagh on that pleasant Saturday afternoon, however, killed 28 people and injured 330 more. Among the victims were members of a group of children visiting from the Irish Republic, some pregnant women, some babies, and a twelve-year-old boy from Spain. Most of those who died were Catholic.

The Pugnacious Peacemaker

David Trimble faced his toughest challenge on October 28, 2000, when members of the Ulster Unionist Party, of which he was head, denounced his leadership. Trimble had agreed to Sinn Fein participation in the Northern Ireland Assembly in exchange for an end to IRA violence. But the IRA did not disarm, and dissident members staged raids. With the power-sharing government at stake, Trimble survived a no-confidence vote with support from only 54 percent of the delegates.

Born in 1944, David Trimble graduated as a lawyer from Queens University, Belfast. Elected to the British Parliament, he became a leader of the small but influential Ulster Unionist bloc. He was known as a "pugnacious advocate" for continued British control over Northern Ireland.

Elected head of the Ulster Unionist Party in 1995, Trimble joined in peace talks, but insisted that the IRA disarm. He broke off talks in February 1996 following a renewal of IRA terrorism, but later rejoined them, playing a major role in reaching the Good Friday Agreement. This led to Trimble being cowinner (with John Hume) of the Nobel Peace Prize in 1998.

Leader of the Ulster Unionist Party David Trimble with his family arriving at The Millennium Dome in Greenwich, London, to celebrate the beginning of the new millennium.

Gerry Adams, who had always refused to comment on or apologize for IRA violence, "condemned" the Omagh bombing "without equivocation." David Trimble, who in the past had always accused Adams and Sinn Fein of responsibility for acts of violence, held his tongue and continued to negotiate with Adams and Hume. Two months after the bombing, Trimble and John Hume won the 1998 Nobel Peace Prize for their hard work and the risks they took in their quest to end violence in Northern Ireland. However, when David Trimble attended the

Sinn Fein President Gerry Adams (left), Social Democratic Party leader John Hume, and First Minister David Trimble (right) pose with President Bill Clinton at the White House on St. Patrick's Day in 2000.

funeral in a Catholic church of three of the children killed at Omagh—two aged twelve and one aged eight—the Orange Order threatened to expel him because a condition of membership is that "you should not countenance by your presence or otherwise any act or ceremony of Popish worship." Trimble answered that he was acting on "precisely those charitable Christian values which are the duty of every Orangeman."

By contrast, a spin-off group calling itself the Orange Volunteers bombed a Catholic-owned bar in Crumlin,

County Antrim. They said that an IRA leader drank there. In fact, eleven of the twelve customers at the time of the attack were Protestants. The Volunteers also announced that they would take action against those IRA members released from British prisons as part of the Good Friday Agreement.

Problems and Progress

The quest for peace continued to be hampered by militants throughout 1999 and 2000. Response to violent actions underlies many of those issues that negotiators still find most difficult to resolve. The IRA, while not directly involved in recent raids, is suspected by the British, and by Ulster Protestants, of being the source of weapons for the Real IRA and other dissident Catholic groups. International groups have made two inspections of IRA weapons sites, but the IRA has opposed further inspections and has refused to give up its weapons until Britain speeds up its closing of military bases in Northern Ireland. British Prime Minister Tony Blair, citing the withdrawal of 3,500 soldiers from Northern Ireland, insists that an obligation to protect local Protestants from IRA dissidents makes it necessary not to cut British forces any further.

Another IRA condition for disarmament has to do with the creation of a new police service to replace the hated Royal Ulster Constabulary. Recommendations laid out by an international commission for a new police force have been so watered down by the British, the IRA claims, that they are unacceptable. A *New York Times* editorial agreed, deploring the lack of a mechanism to investigate "the RUC's past abuses, and weed out guilty officers."

With Catholics sharing power in government thanks to the Good Friday Agreement, Protestant power has

Rebel With a Cause

There was no Nobel Prize for Gerry Adams in 1998 when negotiators of the Northern Ireland question were honored. There could be no agreement without him, but the president of Sinn Fein was too militant to be acclaimed a peacemaker. Adams was a hero to his followers, but to his critics, an unrepentant rebel who supported IRA violence.

Born on October 6, 1948, Gerry Adams grew up in a Catholic working-class neighborhood of Belfast. He worked as a bartender and became active in civil-rights protests in the 1960s. During the 1970s he was jailed by the British several times. He became vice president of Sinn Fein, the political arm of the IRA, in 1973 and president in 1983.

Elected to the British Parliament from 1982 through 1992, Adams refused to take his seat. Nevertheless, he became active in the peace process, brokering the first IRA cease-fire in 1994. In 1999, Adams committed Sinn Fein to "all aspects" of the Good Friday Agreement.

He continued to walk a tightrope in 2001, defending IRA interests while negotiating with the British and the Ulster Unionists.

Sinn Fein President Gerry Adams outside the Houses of Parliament in London in 1996

been eroded. They see the replacement of the RUC by a "Police Service of Northern Ireland" as further severing ties with Great Britain. This once again raises the possibility of reuniting Ulster with the Irish Republic and coming under Catholic rule.

On the other hand, Catholics live in fear of frequent violence by Orange Volunteers and other Protestant paramilitary groups. Recurring marches by the Orange Order through Catholic neighborhoods in many cities of

Northern Ireland often deteriorate into violence. Fanatic leaders like the Reverend Ian Paisely preach a doctrine of violence against Catholics, which is too often followed.

There are also fanatics on the other side. On January 23, 2001, a mortar bomb was fired by IRA dissidents into a British army base in Derry. Scrawled on the launching-plate of the bomb was an abusive message. It was not addressed to a British or Ulster leader. Its target was the Sinn Fein president currently facing off with the British in the peace talks: Gerry Adams.

Less than a week later, in Boston and Chicago, money was being raised to support the Real IRA. Violence costs money. This is as true for the Orange Volunteers as for the Real IRA. With more than 3,600 lives lost since 1969, the question is, how many more people will have to be maimed, or killed, in Northern Ireland before well-meaning donors stop giving money to fuel what both sides call "The Troubles?"

Near the end of 2001, there was new hope for peace in Northern Ireland. This was surprising in view of events earlier in the year. In the wake of the IRA's continued refusal to disarm throughout the spring and summer of 2001, David Trimble, head of the Ulster Unionists, resigned as first minister of the Northern Ireland Assembly. Three other Ulster Unionist members also resigned their government posts in protest against the IRA's refusal to turn in their guns by the June 2001 deadline. Riots in Belfast followed, culminating in assaults by Protestants on Catholic children walking to school. By September, the prospects for peace had never seemed dimmer.

According to *The New York Times*, the September 11, 2001, "attacks on New York and Washington and the subsequent declaration of war on terrorism by President Bush . . . made pariahs of countries and organizations harboring armed guerrillas." Sinn Fein had reason to fear that American supporters would be reluctant to donate any more money to their cause. On October 23, the IRA reversed its long-held position and began dismantling its weapons. Two days later, David Trimble and the three Ulster Unionist members who had resigned announced their intention to rejoin the government. The British began removing military watchtowers and implemented a program of troop withdrawals. Although both Catholic and Protestant extremists oppose these moves toward peace, the mood in Northern Ireland was generally conciliatory and hopeful.

The large majority of both Catholics and Protestants want to live in peace. Realizing that dream has boiled down to settling a handful of major questions. Shall the British relinquish all control over Northern Ireland? Shall hope of reuniting Northern Ireland with the Republic of Ireland be abandoned? Shall the IRA totally disarm itself? Can the militants on both sides be made to halt the raids, bombings, and killings?

Most Protestants recognize that Catholics have been discriminated against, and that the discrimination must end if there is to be peace. Most Catholics understand that after more than five hundred years Protestants have a right to call Northern Ireland their home, and that the Protestants of today are not responsible for the acts of persecution by those who came before them. Both Protestants and Catholics realize that the hotheads who throw the bombs that kill their children are the real enemy. Both Protestants and Catholics want "The Troubles" to end.

Chronology

5th Century A.D.	St. Patrick introduces Christianity into Ireland.
12th Century A.D.	Raids by Anglo-Norman barons from England lead to conquest of Ireland.
16th Century A.D.	Church of England established; Catholicism banned in Ireland; Ulster earls launch eight-year rebellion.
1607	"Flight of the Earls" followed by British seizure of their lands, establishment of the "Ulster Plantation," and migration of Presbyterian Scots to Northern Ireland begins.
1641	Ulster Catholics begin nine-year rebellion against British and Scots.
1650	Oliver Cromwell puts down rebellion, reestablishes harsh British rule.
July 12, 1690	William of Orange's army defeats Irish Catholic forces of King James II at the Battle of the Boyne.
1760–1800	The Industrial Revolution brings major changes to Northern Ireland.
1800	The Act of Union is passed, creating the United Kingdom of Great Britain and Ireland.
1804–1807	Daniel O'Connell leads the Emancipation movement.
1845–1851	The potato famine kills 1.5 million people and provokes small-scale uprisings throughout Ireland.

1869	Anti-Catholic Popery Code laws are repealed.
1881	The Land Act, a reform measure granting relief to Irish tenant farmers, is passed.
1890	The cause of Irish Home Rule suffers a major blow when reformer Charles Parnell's affair with Kitty O'Shea causes a scandal.
1914	As World War I begins, the British Parliament passes Irish Home Rule legislation, but postpones implementation until the war is over.
1916	The Easter Rising in Dublin is brutally put down by the British.
1918	Sinn Fein declares the revolutionary Republic of Ireland; the IRA is born.
1920	The Government of Ireland Act creates a partition between Northern and Southern Ireland.
1921	Michael Collins signs a treaty that leaves Northern Ireland under British rule; Eamon De Valera leads anti-partition forces opposing the treaty; a bloody civil war breaks out.
June 22, 1921	Northern Ireland sets up a parliament with Sir James Craig as prime minister.
Aug. 22, 1922	Collins is assassinated; it is rumored that De Valera gave the order.
May 1923	The civil war ends.
1927	De Valera and other Republicans take the oath of loyalty to the British crown.
1932	De Valera is elected president of the Irish Free State.
1935	Major clashes between Catholics and Protestants in Belfast.
1937	The Irish Free State severs ties with Britain and establishes the Republic of Ireland.
1968–1972	Inspired by the U. S. civil-rights movement, Ulster Catholics stage a series of peaceful protests brutally put down by the Royal Ulster Constabulary and British army.
Jan. 30, 1972	"Bloody Sunday": British paratroopers fire into a crowd of protesters killing fourteen and wounding seventeen.
1972	British abolish Northern Ireland parliament and take over the government.

1973	Catholics boycott a vote to decide if Northern Ireland should remain part of Great Britain.
1976	A major joint Protestant and Catholic peace movement earns the Nobel Prize for Mairead Corrigan and Betty Williams, but fades away as violence grows
1970s–1980s	Ongoing violence between the IRA and Protestant paramilitary groups.
1985	Great Britain and the Republic of Ireland agree to a Republic voice in Ulster affairs.
1990–1992	Talks aimed at returning Northern Ireland to local rule are held, but break down.
1993	Sinn Fein asked to renounce violence and join new peace talks.
Aug. 31, 1994	The IRA announces it will halt military operations.
Feb. 9, 1996	The IRA announces cease-fire is over and sets off a huge bomb in London.
1997	Skillful negotiating by former U. S. Senator George Mitchell results in another IRA cease-fire, and brings Ulster Unionists and Sinn Fein back to the peace table.
1998	The Good Friday Agreement is signed and overwhelmingly approved by voters in Northern Ireland and the Irish Republic.
1998	Ulster Unionist Party leader David Trimble and Catholic Social Democratic and Labour Party chief John Hume are awarded the Nobel Peace Prize.
Aug. 15, 1998	The Real IRA sets off a bomb in Omagh, killing 28 people and injuring 330.
1999–2000	Continuing violence by the Real IRA and the Orange Volunteers.
2000	Standoff between British Prime Minister Tony Blair and Sinn Fein over IRA disarmament, withdrawal of British forces from Ulster, and replacement of Royal Ulster Constabulary
Oct. 28, 2000	Ulster Unionist Party leader David Trimble barely survives a no-confidence vote in the Northern Ireland Assembly.
Jan. 23, 2001	Real IRA bomb sends abusive message to Sinn Fein president Gerry Adams.

Spring and Summer 2001	David Trimble resigns as first minister of the Northern Ireland Assembly; three other Ulster Unionist members also resign their government posts; riots in Belfast lead to assaults by Protestants on Catholic children walking to school.
October 2001	IRA begins dismantling weapons; David Trimble and three Ulster ministers announce intention to rejoin government; British implement troop withdrawals.

For Further Reading

Ardagh, John. *Ireland and the Irish.* London: Hamish Hamilton, 1994.

Fraser, TG. *Ireland in Conflict: 1922–1998.* New York: Routledge, 2000.

Holland, Jack. *Hope Against History: The Course of Conflict in Northern Ireland.* New York: Henry Holt & Company, 1999.

Holliday, Laurel (editor). *Children of "the Troubles": Our Lives in the Cross-Fire of Northern Ireland.* New York: Washington Square Press, 1998.

Taylor, Peter. *Behind the Mask: The IRA and Sinn Fein.* New York: TV Books Inc., 1997.

Woodham-Smith, Cecil. *The Great Hunger.* New York: Old Town Books, 1989.

Index